RECONNAISSANCE

RECONNAISSANCE

Anne Higgins

Texture Press
Norman, Oklahoma

Texture Press
Managing Editor: Susan Smith Nash, Ph.D.
1108 Westbrooke Terrace
Norman, OK 73072
E-mail: texturepress@beyondutopia.com

Author photograph by Michael Hoover, used by permission.
Cover design by Arlene Ang
Book design by Texture Press

ISBN-13: 978-0692300046
ISBN-10: 069230004X

CONTENTS

BINOCULARS

THE HUE OF MY SHOE

*..scientists at the University of Arizona found, on a sampling
of 26 shoes worn by test subjects for three months or longer:
bacteria that cause blood infections, urinary tract and wound
infections, intestinal tract infections... which the subjects
tracked into the carpets and flooring of their homes...*
-Baltimore Sun, *5/6/08*

Today with new eyes I viewed
black rubber on the soles of my shoes
carrying constellations of Klebsiella pneumoniae,
condominiums of pseudomonas luteola,
whole civilizations of E. Coli.
The smooth black of my soles
absorbs the other colors:
the hue of robin guano,
squashed earthworm,
powdered mulch,
dust of chlorine and cholera
from all the floors of all the public toilets
of ten years of visiting.
I heard my mother saying that
you had to eat a peck of dirt before you die.

BINOCULARS

Catering to the desire to see
further than is possible
when using the naked eye,
the desire to see the
Yellow-breasted Chat
who chuckles in the Cape May sun
from a distant Post Oak.
Binoculars present the opportunity.
What you choose to look through
makes all the difference.

Objective lens,
ocular lens,
Porro Prism gathers enough light,
provides precision,
and even better,
eye relief.

My father bought these for me
thirty years ago.
Rubber eyepieces now crumble
from age, sweat, heat,
skin oil,
bug spray.
Still, they make the light rays parallel, offer
stereoscopic vision,
surround sound seeing.

The Yellow-breasted Chat
glows buttery gold
in the sunlight,
appearing eight times
closer .
I see the lustful glint
in his beady black eyes.

An Active and Personal Devil

It has been reported by the New York Times...*that as technology increases, more and more people are going to believe in an active and personal devil.*
-Miller Williams

The door was wood, with peeling paint
and a china doorknob
white,cracked, spider web of
black cracks, but not chapped.
The door was closed,
but not too hard to open.
The devil sat behind the door,
hunched over a table, hiding.
She was thin and young.
I asked her why and she looked at me
and did not answer.
I left her, but left the door ajar.
I felt in my shoulders
two red tomatoes, like organs of the body,
red balls, and furry.
They tell me to watch out,
that I'm letting my heart go.
Soon I see a small white closet
with a black tile floor.
In back of it waits a
thin cherry door, a hoard of
copper pipes.
I see the door leads to another country,
backed up by a stone
In a deep summer forest.
Laminate, I think, no,
Lamia.

COMMUTER

Radio lady on Time saver traffic
Speaks her short words to me:
Heads up!
Road Work
Rubber Neck
Turn Lane
Bail Out
Medi-Vac
All Lanes Blocked.

From the Drive Thru,
Eat in the Car, Pay at the Pump,
What short words
Will bail me out?

On the Washington Beltway
I deplore the curves,
the way it moves the Mormon Tabernacle
from one side to the other.
I detest the ramps, the way it spews my car
directly into ongoing traffic.
I loathe the merges,
the way the Virginia side
squeezes from five lanes
to two,
backing up cars like
beans in a clogged kitchen drain.
I condemn the speeders who ride my rear,
those in huge SUVs
who cut in front of me
like large black sharks,
talking on cellphones.
I dread the stalled bus,
the road construction,
the dead eighteen wheeler in the middle lane,
and most of all,
the fallout onto Seven Corners,
the Dante Local.

BLIND SPOT

In the car, out to the left, it lurks.
Something blocks my view
I think I'm clear to move
and suddenly! Someone's there!

Something blocks my view-
It's out to the left,where I can't see,
and suddenly someone's there.
His angry horn attacks.

Out to the left where I can't see
until almost too late-
His angry horn attacks.
My heart slams through my ribs.

Until almost too late,
something blocks my view
but passes me this time.
I think I'm clear to move.

THE ESCORT MODIFIER

Lured by my love of grammar,
intrigued by my ad in the personals,
dressed correctly in spiffy suit,
he always accompanies me.
He's accommodating, flexible,
sometimes intrusive,
often distracting.
Frequently superfluous, he comes
often bearing
unnecessary qualifications
like boxes of candy I don't need,
fattening, often cheap,
candy I don't even like.

Sometimes a Boy

Sometimes a boy
turns up like a large turnip
in my classroom.

Sometimes he smirks
like a salamander.

Sometimes he gives me
the blank stare
of a mackerel
that tells me
I'm still
the Osprey.

TWO FEET FROM A FLICKER

Two feet from my seat at my desk
to the windowsill where
on the other side of the glass
a Flicker feasts on the seed and nut bar
I have provided for my entertainment
and his nourishment.
If he sees me, he doesn't care.
I try not to move too much.
I can see his ears,
a slight bulge under his feathers.
I can see the sun shining off his black
eyes that are all pupil.
His left hand clutches the seed bar.
His long beak, longer than a Red Belly's,
pokes into the block of seed and nuts and raisins.
His tongue fine as a hairpin
touches it.
He wears a cherry red cap on the nape of his neck,
black raindrop shapes on his cheeks,
a black necklace on his throat and gold ermine on his chest,
and as he fends off an approaching Bluejay,
His gold shafts flare out on the inside of his wings.
Oh, fifteen whole minutes I've had with you,
my beautiful customer!

THE DETECTIVE

Dreamed last night
that I was the main character in
an Agatha Christie mystery in
an English village garlanded with climbing roses
thatched roofs, wild bird calls in the night.
The murderer turned out to be an
ancient woman,
thin, cottony haired, hands like talons.
I was clad only in my summer bathrobe,
long, taffeta, plaid peach and white,
not chenille, but plisse,
and my lover, that skinny red-headed boy,
wrapped his arms around me in the morning light,

and maybe we were married.
We waited in the sunny kitchen
with three other villagers
for the police,
Detective Superintendent Barnaby,
urbane ,ironic and soft spoken,
to arrive.

THIRTEEN WAYS OF LOOKING AT A POETRY CLASS

Pointy toed shoes tap
tile sticky with
spilled stories.

Brown boots ready for
dressage.
Inside , the feckless feet.

Purple cotton arms
hug each other,
contemplates the words
on the screen.

Twists brown hair into a knot
and lets it fall back
listless to the shoulders.

Grey cardigan shivers,
writes about mongrels.

Strokes its young goatee,
counts syllables
on its fingers.

Knit shirt with pink sequins
hunches muff, writes
love poem.

Shoulders roll in
rusty jacket,

twirls the pen
like a baton.

Black and white striped
Maxi Dress
drinks coffee,
writes about mirrors.

Blue Jeans Jacket
faded, sleeves rolled up
to a baseball ballad.

Coughs a deep
devoted cough,
curls its
furry feet.

Blue school jersey
registers the drilling of heating system
repair people next door,
thinks about dentists and motorcycles.
The sounds make their way
into its notebook.

Head with the gold knit cap surveys
the stains on the carpet,
writes of oil slicks
on the sands of Louisiana.

KAELLING (DANISH)

We have no word for the woman in Harris-Teeter
who screams at her children,
the grubby four year old and his jumping brother,
who run up and down the cereal aisle.
She curses at them and smacks the
four year old on his bottom as the brother jumps up and down,
so that now they are all three of them yelling.
In Danish, she is called a Kaelling,
which sounds more musical
Than the sound she's making
in the cereal aisle.

At Monticello Dam, California

Sink hole of secrets,
draw hole of subterfuge,
spillway,
tunnel funnel of
water swallowing water
in the middle of water,
shining grey circle
in the satin calm
opens
when dam is full to overflowing,
when water needs draining
from the reservoir of tears.
Swallowing 14,000 cubic feet of water
every second-
humans carved,
humans control
this great thirst.

Not like the blue holes in the oceans
not made by human hands,
the great blue hole off the coast of Belize-
turquoise skin surrounds
night sky navy eye
brimming tears
bottomless cornea.

LIKE THE EYES OF INSECTS

LIKE THE EYES OF INSECTS

Insects solve the day-night tradeoff
with their seven-faceted eyes.
The fruit fly, even the hated housefly
know how to peer into
the solution.

Like the eyes of an insect,
the seven facets of the eyes of God,
the seven faceted lamp
the caulkers of their seams
the caulkers of your seems
traders for your good,
traitors for your goods,
the warriors within you,
the great crowd within you.

Hearth cake overturned
a heart cake ,
now the end is on you,
the envelope of the abyss,
licked and thrown into the blue box.

BLUE-WINGED TEAL

Small dabbling duck,
wallow in freshwater ,
mince your steps on the sticky fronds
of April,
rest your blue bill on your speckled chest
like a dignified dowager,
looking down her nose.

Fashionable in your touches of sapphire
on breast and wings,
your color is more blue than
what the paint store calls teal,

something more moody than
turquoise,
more matte than satin.

CROCOSIMA

Named Lucifer, she rides her curving stem
Rococo red glad mimic in the shade
Seems rare as orchid, skating on her blade
Of stiff hard green, her color sings a hymn
To all those corms whose offspring number them
Among the stars, prolific garden trades
Because they crowd and choke the flower beds.
Late summer crows sway scarlet in the light
Of slanting sun on slender arching branch
Named Lucifer, those thousand bug sized crows
Of red, assembled bold and bright
Like sailboats getting ready for their launch,
Like poison berries no one ever knows.

Rules for Action in the Garden

Sidle up to the garden
and speak to it.
Applaud the crocuses.
Kiss the rose.
Push the tulips.
Pray about the old blueberry bush:
oh garden god, just let it die;
I don't have the heart to dig it up.
Caress the evergreen now taller than you,
which you planted when it came to your knee.
It will sigh with pleasure at the memory of your hand,
the violence of its uprooting and replanting,
hurt of the dirt pushed around it,
ecstasy of comforting water.
Yell at the robins who eat the sweet cherries
before you reach them.
Prostrate yourself in the grass,
with its thatch and uneven patches,
weeds and moss and mole tunnels.

GROUND COVER

Still the weeds show up
like noxious visitors
in the midst of the intentions
of the ground cover.
Chickweed, Crabgrass,
Thistle,Dandelion,
Johnsongrass,
moving in on me
when I am too weak
to fight them.
Wild Strawberries,
Vines thin as florist wires
Woven through the ajuga:
pull one, pull the other.
Take off the gloves
And get those bare fingers
Poking it to the ground
To feel the root.

My previous deployments
of Ajuga, Lily of the Valley,
Hosta,
cannot prevent their sprouting.

Now I find another invader
I actually planted.
Disguised as a benign resident,
Bishop's Weed,
with its lovely variegated leaves,
gallops out of my control,
encroaches on the Pinks,
smothers the Lamb's Ears.

THE VIOLENCE OF APRIL

Stalking the garden,
lily of the valley spikes
hurdle Spring.

Viburnum grips air-
intense perfume lures,
claims attention.

THE RETICENCE OF JANUARY

Pungent throaty flute–
Carolina Wren arrives
on the windowsill.

Snowplow scrapes below.
Sparrows grouse in huddled boxwood huts,
sleep disturbed again.

OCTOBER IN EMMITSBURG

Sun backlights the gold trees.
Suddenly they jump up,
out of the dark
at the end of daylight savings time.
Moon rides the sky,
hovers over the mountain.

It's inner trickery
to love the fall.

BUZZ POLLINATION

Bumblebees live deep underground all winter.
In the spring they come out singing.
They are mated females, known as queens,
the only survivors from last year.
They favor the shooting star, a wildflower clotted with pollen,
an early bloomer.
She sends vibrations through the flower.
The shooting star shakes her downward hanging flower,
lets loose that pollen,
thrilled and ecstatic.
It's called "Buzz Pollination"

Black lamp eyes of the worker bee
concentrates on the spitting gold stitches
on the face of the shooting star.
Brittle glass wings,
hairy thorax,
delicate feet touch down.

THE BROODY HEN

You can identify a broody hen by her Zen-like gaze and deep,
wary settling into the nest."
-Mother Earth News

Born with her back to sin,
oblivious to turbulence,
the Buff Orpington's gone broody.
She's for warming those eggs, all of them.
She dreams of hatching them, raising them,
protecting them, teaching them to find food.

She mutters, growls when approached,
leaves the nest once a day
to eat and defecate.
She'll sit on everyone else's eggs too, but
she won't lay anymore herself
while brooding.

Some hens insist on being broody,
persistently broody.
She's one who won't quit brooding.

She fluffs out her peachy camel feathers
on a near permanent basis
in order to raise her body temperature
to incubate all eggs all the time,
to keep the chicks warm.

She peers at the farmer from the corner of her eye
suspicious, ready to attack,
huge, fluffy, formidable.

ALOUETTE

Oak as stiff as pride
Bark so sharp it cried
Nuthatch holds those creases tight
So the year lets go
Splashing into snow,
So the day gives way to night.

Skylark stays year round
Lifts the air with sound
Sparrow brown in English towns
Heard before it's seen
Yearns for open green
Populations losing ground.

KNOWING AGAIN

IRISH FAMILIES

Doing penance for our sins,
offering it up,
we're fond of company,
whiskey,
and Jansenism.
We tell this joke on ourselves:
Irish Alzheimer's?
You forget everything
but the grudges.

Our folk dance features
deft and flying feet,
while the rest of the body
freezes rigid, expressionless.

That's so Irish,
we say of each other's
verbal innuendo,
ambiguity,
interruptions,
non-sequitors.

We're talking Irish –
masters of verbal obscurity,
group conversation as
double talk
obfuscation.

What a word that is!
The art of obvious fuses,
fusty effusions,
indirection,
bombastic, belligérant, sentimental,
a terror to our enemies,
a joy to our friends,
a jig of mystery
at home.

COROT BLUE

puckered with clouds,
Damask wards off rain
Father Hopkins, lick ink into my pen
Shake blue over paper.

My parents' wedding day
Cold and blustery in 1944
Outside the rectory of Saint Agnes Parish
In the brittle afternoon sun.
My mother holding her hat on her head,
Shivering in her new suit.
No wedding gown for the non-Catholic ceremony
Of thirtysomethings in the rectory.
My father dapper happy in a new dark suit
So glad she said yes.

LENAPE PARK, 1959

Eight years old,
sleek as a seal
in her shiny wet swimsuit,
She climbs the ladder
to the high dive.

Ten feet up, balanced by thick August air,
She slowly bends to see,
depths down, the glacier pool

The sun throws pools of satin
over the water
in the early evening.
Distant radio plays
mandolin music –
You're sure to fall in love...

She thinks of pirates,
of tumbles down stairs,
of flying.
A quick feeling like a leaf,
then splash.

AT LITTLE FLOWER CAMP

At Little Flower Camp
in the summer of 1957,
first time away from home,
She's nine,
coddled.
Hates how cold the cabin gets at night,
hates the cold twelve stall toilets,
hates having to go swimming in the cold pool.
But the first night,
before bed,
the counselors herded them
into the large pine gathering room.
All of the campers from six to twelve,
little girls,
on the benches facing the stage.
In the dark, the singing began:
Tell me why.....
the stars do shine...
tell me why...
the ivy twines..
tell me why...
the sky is so blue...
tell me , Little Flower,
why do we love you?
All those girl voices,
trailing off the "Why" in a swooping arc,
and the three part harmony...
all those little girls singing
and their voices took her
somewhere she had never gone,
 the only child,
from the quiet house of grownups.

HEARING YESTERDAY

Hearing "Yesterday" the first time - 1964-
my bedroom in the house on Everhart Street,
I was fifteen.
February night.
At night my radio could tune into Boston.
When I turned it on, the song was just beginning -
Three syllables down the scale,
cello droning behind them.
Throat tightened, legs loosened.
My favorite song forever.

Forty-five years later,
troubles not so far away .
One long lost love called in 1971
better to laugh in the desert
than cry by the creek,
but I could not move to the desert.

Today I live by that creek again –
cornered by circumstance,
shedding my escape fantasies,
singing with Ringo
No no no no I don't smoke it no more...

By the creek,
today tenuous as a spider web,
unpredictable as fire.

I believe in yesterday,
which does not change,
where John Lennon still walks
unaware
out the door of the Dakota.

Another song says don't stop thinking about tomorrow.
But I believe in yesterday.
Another song says the landslide brought me down...

and I'm getting older, too,
so I believe in yesterday.

APOLOGY POEM

Brenda Lee sings *I'm Sorry* in her halting voice,
voice like a boy's, choking low like a tomboy's voice,
harsh, halting, timbre changing,
please accept my apology....

Who's sorry now?
I'm sorry for the time I ran over the rabbit on the country road,
for never asking my mother about her childhood,
for not going to the eye doctor for five years,
until it was too late
sorry for all the times it was too late.

I'm sorry for selfish reasons,
for words that got me in trouble,
for words held back.

Sorry for negligence too global to mention.

Sorry I don't want to list any more.
Wishing I could pack up
all the sorrows
in some overlooked locker
in the far corner of a bus station
in a desert outpost.
Sorry I wished for that.

GREATEST HITS OF 1948

I'm Looking over a Four Leaf Clover
That I overlooked before luck
had anything to do with
My Happiness.
Hydrogen bombs were readied;
Truman was elected,
Israel became a state
in that year I was born,
a year I used to think was notable
only for my birth.
In that year, only
Cool Water
would soothe my yearning lips,
as my mother oared me away on a
Slow Boat to China,
telling me I was her
Ramblin Rose,
telling me that , even as Levittown
was rising from piles of debris,
The Best Things in Life are Free.

EVERYONE'S GONE TO THE MOON

Rousseau painted the gypsy sleeping under the full moon
in dazzling deep cobalt sky ,
dreaming face like a totem serene
in a dream of lute music.
Pipe song,
grazing wildeyed lion
huge behind him
standing guard over his dreams
bedhead mane stiff with moonlight
eyes wild white balls and staring corneas
tail at the alert

1969 and I'm serving drinks
at the Kennett Square Country Club,
so glad to be 21 and able to serve drinks.
The golfers at the bar stare with wild white eyeballs
at the tiny moonman in his white spacesuit
moving jerkily on the cratered surface
faceless, the glass in his helmet shining back
the distant earth
and I notice it without much excitement,
immersed as I am in being 21 years old,
thinking this will happen a lot
from now on.
In my dreams.

A Wild Séance of Delight and Cunning

Picture this:
Ten college seniors sit around an old wooden table in a dark bar
on a rainy night.
They are drinking beer – the only alcoholic beverage served in
this bare bar.
The one who paints pictures of nightmares
and charcoal sketches of gnarled trees
wraps his hands around his glass, glares
at the others, whispering
Picture this:
and he tells a story about the murder of a mailman.
He tells this story in a hushed, irrevocable voice.
While they listen, the other nine
picture the story
while part of their minds whisper to themselves:
Picture this:
the storyteller – he will be a great artist.
Another among us will be a famous novelist.
Another, a millionaire songwriter.
Another , President of the United States,
another, a great actor.

Picture this:
In fifteen years, not one of them knows the whereabouts
of any of the others.
In thirty years,
one is dead of leukemia
one is dead of AIDS,
one is a billionaire businessman,
one is a high school art teacher,
one works for the IRS,
one has five children,
one has moved to Ireland,
one has joined the convent.
In forty years, the other two have disappeared
beyond any search engine.
The dark bar has become

a picturesque, pricey restaurant.

Picture This
call back the worlds –
a wild séance of delight and cunning.

PERDITA

If I had a daughter, I would name her Perdita.
Of course, the time when I could have a daughter is long
gone.
But that name, the lost one, calls to me tonight.
Like Anita, and Rita, and Jacquita, Lolita, Florita, it is Latin and
lovely
but it's lost, too.
So my lost eggs, long ago shriveled up,
and lost nest, more recently fried by radiation.
Perdita, your name wouldn't go well with my last name,
or the names of any of the men I would have married,
but you are the lost one,
the invisible one,
the one I never would have had the patience
to toilet train, to leash train like a puppy,
to train like a stubborn adolescent.
Never meant to be a mother,
today, more than old enough to be a grandmother,
I think of long lost tempests,
and you.

ORIENTED

My mother, though almost blind, almost deaf,
no longer able to care for herself,
is oriented.
She knows me, knows my name,
answers questions with perspicacity.
She's oriented.
The word comes from Middle English, from Old French,
from the Latin *oriens*, for the rising sun.
She is aligned with the rising sun,
familiar with family,
with her position, with her situation,
where she sits, in her wheelchair.
Actually, she's occidented.
Related to *occidere*: to fall – of the sun –
but she has fallen, broken her hip,
fallen out of bed.
Now she slides herself out of the wheelchair,
gently lowers herself to the floor.
The sun falls, and she's set.

At the Foot Doctor

She's afraid to cut her toenails anymore,
afraid she'll cut her toe,
cause blood and weeks of limping
maybe worse.

Her fellow waiters seem
more afflicted and defeated,
hobbling in slippers, on walkers,
guided by adult children
of workaholics.
They shift in the hard seats.
The waiting room cramped
as a shoe one size too small.

What it must be to have his job!
All day with other's feet in his hands,
shaving off calluses, kneading sore
 worn out fascia,
comforting those tired, twisted servants
who balk at any more work.

PHYSICS FOR POETS

The realm of quantum theory is the very small-
Relativity deals with the very large or the very fast-
Gravity is the central mystery of our created universe.

I see the man falling the falling man from the World Trade
    Center.
Terminal velocity-
I don't understand it, but
I hear his body hit the roof of the Atrium,
 hear the shocked cries of the people there that day.

I think of Acceleration in terms of objects... my car, hurtling
down Route 95...
In the absence of resistance,
all falling bodies experience
the same constant acceleration.
That falling man,
that man falling head first, arms close at his sides
in his business suit,
from the World Trade Center
in the absence of resistance.

What does death smell like?
There is an inherently human smell
Though the Japanese say that we Americans smell like butter
And it repels them...
This inherently human smell
Only when this smell is in its extreme form, in decay,
We notice it.

The smell of death – a sweet syrupy smell
A meaty odor – hamburger that's just about to go bad...
Circling the drain, a term from nurses...
A corpse smell in a living person...

But the falling man did not have time to smell...
Within the hour he was vaporized.

DEBRIEFING MAGRITTE

THERE IS NO CONNECTION

There is no connection between
the cabernet in the whiskey glass
and the coffee in the toothbrush glass,
or between the French fries for supper
and the pear for breakfast,
or between the golden six in the evening sun
and the rain cascade of six in the morning,
or between the Baccalaureate Mass at five in the evening
and the Funeral Mass at eleven in the morning,
or between the cloud and the stone
which hover over the ocean
in Magritte's painting Les Idees Claires.

No connection
Between Magritte and Hopkins
Between my ruminations
And my gesticulations

Nothing but inscape
Linking loss and land.

MAGRITTE PAINTS THE COMPANIONS OF FEAR

Five owls blooming
in the granite of
nightmares,
the garden of
preoccupations:
Short-eared hard of hearing thunder.
Great Horned rage swoops down on silent wings.
Barred blind, hit by a car as he dives for the rabbit.
Barn withholds his screeching objections.
Saw-whet seeks water to drown in.
Perch together on a cloudy summit
nearby.

ANGRY ENOUGH TO DIE

God found Jonah and asked him, "Have you reason
to be angry?"
"I have reason to be angry," Jonah answered God,
"Angry enough to die."

My shady gourd plant is gone,
my cucumber, my castor,
under which I sheltered,
within which I heed.
Now I grope for the sky, that false mirror,
hot burning my skin,
skin cancer blossoming like a dandelion.
I have reason to be angry.

I have still not tasted
the flavor of my tears.
Still I mirror
Magritte's painting,
where the sand yellow leaf blossoms a watchful hawk,
though the leaf borer makes lace of his breast
so the grey sea gapes though it.
Angry enough to die.

I'll eat and drink till my heart chars.
Till that sunset burns clear through.

He is not speaking.
I lower my concrete mask
and listen.

WORKSHOP IN THE GARDEN, BRUSSELS

Purple-leafed plum tree flowers pink
outside Maison Magritte.
Tall hedge round the garden,
glimpse of cherry tree inside.
Deep roof, porch overlooking the garden
just big enough for one.
Long narrow garden, not too many flowers.
mostly grass,
narrow sidewalk down the middle.
Within the shed at the far end of the garden
Magritte paints.
Paints and signs wallpaper
to make money to support the other paintings.
Roses on the wallpaper,
gardens in his mind.
 purpose like wind.

IN MAGRITTE I CAN FIND NO STRAWBERRIES

In Magritte I can find no strawberries,
though in Belgium, in June, he must have had
them, luscious, feeding them to Georgette in the afternoon.
Perhaps they sat upon the step
or watched the summer out the window.
Perhaps he saw her face unveiled as no other,
perhaps he told her you are mine
as they fingered the strawberries on plates in their laps,
as they sat by the sea water glistening.
He did not yet see fractures in the sunlight.
He did not yet see blood in the sugar.
He did not yet see the veiled face of the other,
or eggs in a cage at the feast,
or the hat, the feet, the nightmare on the wall.

MAGRITTE REFLECTS ON THE THINGS OF THIS WORLD

What I love about the tuba is its thighs.
What I hate about small bells is their smirk.
What I love about the door is the cloud it lets in.
What I hate about the eye is its false mirror.
What I love about twilight is its color
What I hate about twilight is its shadow empire.
What I love about curtains is their exhibitionism
What I hate about green apples is their intrusiveness.
Good faith, I have found, is not a pipe floating in front of my face;
Good faith is a bird's nest resting safe on an open ledge.

MADAME MAGRITTE RUMINATES ON SYNTAX

Syntax:
how he puts his world in order...
how he forms images from words.
Though he met me at the botanical garden in Brussels,
he paints me naked, lying on my back,
a large conch shell balanced on my flat midsection.
This artist/model dance enfolds us.
A halo of objects appears in the sky
around me:
grey glove, lighted candle, olive leaf,
dove, key, scrap of paper
on which is written "vague."
He paints me naked, standing, turning slightly
like the Venus de Milo,
but red, beside red curtains, my red shadow.
He paints me blue, a dream figure.
He paints me holding his pipe.

MADAME MAGRITTE DESCRIBES HER DOMICILE

We may have lived in God's salon,
a brick house in the suburbs
in bourgeois Belgium.
We argued over the color scheme.
I preferred earthy browns
for the doors, the stairs, the paneling,
but he chose electric blue for the lounge,
lime green for our bedroom,
salmon pink for the dining room,
the room in which he painted every day.
How many returns to the flavor of tears?
I learned to live with the smell of oils
and turpentine.
How many returns to my body half in blue?
How many variations of pipes and tubas?

Even after our short sojourn in Paris,
where my husband decided to paint ideas,
and where Breton asked me to remove it,
I still wore a crucifix around my neck.

Madame Magritte asks her husband in bed

Who is the young girl eating the bird?
You painted her in 1926, and again, twenty years later.
The first time, you called it "Girl Eating a Bird (Pleasure)"
The second time, you called it "Pleasure."
She is not our daughter.
We have no daughter.
Who is the young girl eating the bird?
Her eyes are half-closed, drowsy with pleasure.
Her tongue lingers on the broken breast,
blood on her white lace collar.
In 1926, her hair is black.
In 1946, her hair is light brown.
Is this image the one which makes you retch in the night?
Who is the young girl eating the bird?
The soul only knows that it is hungry.
The other birds crowd around,
calling Horror! Horror!
The soul only knows that it is hungry.
This is the image that makes you shudder,
calling in your sleep
calling Pleasure! Pleasure!

MAGRITTE DESCRIBES RECONNAISSANCE WITHOUT END

Having recognized each other
as someone we have previously seen,
we remember that recognition
in biochemistry,
my response to his substance
based on the reciprocal fit of
a portion of our molecular shapes...
my shadow, my twin,
Raphael to my Tobias,
he joins me.
We rise above the meadow,
inspecting our country for the presence
of enemy installations,
exploring the bright summer map
lying under our mutual gaze.

INTERROGATIONS

IMPLICATIONS

O ANTIPHONS

1

O Magritte sky
over the dead college,
over the government installation
between snowstorms at sunset,
classroom buildings black shoulders
trees creaking butlers in high relief,
bring me an illusion of reprieve.

2

O key of Rilke
where you wait for me
in the pages of the love poems,
O key of C, solid, predictable, yet sliding into
the key of see, often blurry, often double,
barely a quay of sea for me,
tenuous, untethered ,
loose on the wide ocean
of your mercy,
mer
si
merci.

3

O seal of our yearning
glued on the long blue envelope
of sky,
Ciel of our yearning,
grey, mushy today in winter rain,
keep the ink of my prayer
from fade or blood.

4

O long night
full cold moon,
draw me like the sea,
draw me like Magritte paints you
peering through the wrought iron tree.
O Duende,
when I sing with you, no one can qualm,
no one can calm,
no one can come dancing to the dark sound
without feeling your pull on their tides.

5

O gathering light,
receiving light,
ours, ocelli,
theirs, ommatidia,
Who opens the insects
to navigate the world,
finally, late this year, in
mid-November, when
strangely green leaves still stand on the pin oak,
on the mild still day,
at last , a ladybug
sails her way to my window screen,
A fly taxis in for a landing
on the lip of my cup.
Their semper cells –
crystalline cones under the eye lens –
always vigilant,
gathering light.
O facets,
oh cell's eye,
oh my tidings awake,
graciously give me that
faceted
facile receiver!

6

O Route of Jesse
through the desert
of dessert,
foretold by sage
mint and rue, too.
Streets of severance,
tendrils twining on my ankles,
bring me down, holy holly,
bind me, blind me, clutching ivy,
map my angry trip
through the muck of humility.

7

O manual, laboring handbook,
gladden the work of our hands.
We wait for peace,
but terror comes instead.
What factory fashioned the
slashing shrapnel?

Emanate
manual light, new elevation,
elicit handmade candles,
bread, bowls,
chairs,
decoys.
Carpenter, potter, baker,
emit manual glory.

WERE YOU THERE?

Everything must change.
Put yourself on any road, and something will show itself to you.

*

Seeing with glasses the first time,
I looked across the street and saw each
leaf on the tree in the rainy October afternoon,
each leaf significant and clear,
each leaf straining for its clarity in the October air.
Specific, yellow, red ,brown and green,
sharp and present.
Even the meanest, most rain beaten leaf
speaks.

*

My last apartment had a bay window,
high ceilings, shutters,
and polished wood floors.
It was like a small ballroom
On the round wood table, a vase
with one tawny pink peace rose,
unfolded in the afternoon sun.

*

I have a way of seeing through my hand.
A silent dark world running parallel to this one
where we stand upon the lawn
and watch the bright stars
dancing overhead.
The air is thick with voices,
as the students write,
one pen writing in the other's ghost.

*

Without my glasses I have two right hands
twin figure skaters as they hold a pen

so I must touch to see which one is real.
The morning dove speaks deep within her throat.
The river flows by like a giant' s dream,
and if I dipped my hand in, what would come?

*

An ordinary gesture
carries tremendous weight,
hands on my neck and in my hair.

Whose wealth do I want?
Whose power do I want?
Whose name do I want in my mouth?

*

Everything was spilled.
Now I am not there again.
I am somewhere clean and orderly,
where everything happens on the inside,
where it can't be seen
in a long anonymous
interval
of paper towels and long hallways.
I remember the years
vivid with stains,
witnesses to messiness,
where everything was out of place,
everything was touch, everything was spilled.

*

I was somewhere else,
swinging on a swing
in the cold November afternoon, sick of watching
the funeral on television.

*

The weekend of Woodstock,
I was at a wedding
in a yellow striped circus tent

on an elegant lawn,
a glassed in world,
champagne glasses and butlers, white linen napkins.

*

When the plane disappeared into the building,
orange chrysanthemum of death
and catastrophe,
I cancelled my trip to the discount store,
watched numbly the man dive headfirst
to the pavement.

*

It was not before my time,
but it was not in my place.
Just don't ask me to touch those wounds.
They will stain me with your passion
worse than mulberries,
worse, worse than wild blackberries,
worse even than black walnuts,
and I cannot look at my hands like that.

*

Wine has an undercurrent running through its taste
which makes it wine.
You can see lights through it. There are lights in its taste.

*

I remember
before I went to school, when I was three,
visiting my mother's ancient aunt
in the Masonic home,
in Elizabethtown Pa.
My father and I walked the foggy
misty gardens.
Many steps,
smell of boxwood.

How does boxwood smell?
Sharp as goldfinch comments,
intimate as bodies close up, crunchy and green,

dark green, that's how boxwoods smell.
And we heard the sad murmur of the mourning doves,
flutelike and saying,
everyone dies, everyone gets old,
most of us get blind.
In the dark hemlock of age,
arbor vitae of love,
blue spruce of winter,
boxwood of borders,
a name that means twin.

I don't want to put my fingers
into the holes in your hands,
and even less do I want to put my hand
into the wound in your side
that speaks death to me like
a misplaced mouth.
I will be glad to say that I believe you are back
from the dark,
and I will be glad to say I believe them
when they tell me
they have seen you.

FIVE WORDS I NEVER USE

Five words I never use:
paper, nail, whiskey, jam, vomit.
Paper
smooth, blank,
inviting, absorbent, clean
pen, ink cut, metal
incising, splicing, splitting
sharp , shiny
scissors.

Nail, bend the end back
Lest sharpness
Tear the flesh
Of the young Great Dane
As he scales the fence.

Whiskey, liquid gold
Inoculator, immolater,
Turn my cousin's heart
And liver to leather.

Jam, not raspberry
But traffic,
But pushing the large puzzle piece
Into the too small spot.

Vomit, *vomito* in Italian,
Vomir in French, *Kotze* in German,
In Spanish, *Lanzar*,
To dispossess.

INCREMENTAL LOSSES

A thumping on the road – relentless noise –
The marching army carried such a noise.

The soldiers on the road to Gettysburg –
Did they become accustomed to the noise?

Dust rising on the waves of summer heat,
The snort of horses coughing up the noise.

Prepared to lose their hands, their eyes, their breath,
But never losing all that thunderous noise.

The weepers follow, purple-faced and numb-
Did they become accustomed to the noise?

A soldier falling in Afghanistan
Is sure to hear the same relentless noise.

NAME RETRIEVAL

It's been happening for a while
but still it frustrates.
I see the girl's face – a student 10 years back…
What is her name? After a while it appears:
Jennifer –
But the last name? It eludes me.
I start associating: two syllables
maybe three,
near the front of the alphabet…
not an Irish name, maybe English –
an English City…
almost…
Finally I catch it: Leeds!
and where did she come from?
a town in New Jersey…
Does it end in "burg" or "ville"?
Chatham!
Write it down
so you don't lose it again.
Like a tiny chip of eggshell
floating in albumen,
so hard to remove,
so is her name
from my tangled brain.

Something Indistinctly Remembered

What scares me
is what lurks around the next corner
of the dark street.
Don't Look Now,
the name of the most frightening film …
red on the watercolor,
red on the stained glass window,
red raincoat floating on the drowned child
in the pond at the end of the garden.
Peripheral vision
around the edge
feral,
for all,
perilous pearl.

ANOTHER BLIND BEGGAR

I who live in Lie Castle
call to you from my spellbound eyes!
a grey footprint in the center of my vision,
a grey cat sits in the center of the field.

If you can interpret the portents of earth and sky,
if you can read the grains of ice on the car window,
and see helicopters in the clouds,
shrapnel in the snow,
blood in the sunset on the sidewalk,
throw me off the bridge
before burned bodies hang from its turrets.

THE LITTLE DEER

after Frida Kahlo

Ten arrows like daffodil stalks
arranged in a strange bouquet,
stiff with their glut of blood.
I'm leaping,
all four feet in the air,
floating above the lane,
broken branch behind me.

I see you,
my shooter.

WHAT I CANNOT WATCH

Even at eight years of age,
I walked out of *Old Yeller*
because the faithful dog had rabies
and the father was going to shoot him.

The mystery of myself
unable to watch,
unable even to read the scene
when the man beats the horse
in *The Brothers Karamazov,* or in
Edgar Sawtelle,
when the unwavering
eyes of the trusting old dog
watch the adored boy leave him.

Who are these horses and dogs to me
that I cannot watch,
when unblinking, I watch horror films,
murder mysteries,
shootings on TV,
nightly news footage of
dead Iraqi faces?

FIRE IN THE ANGELS

In fifth grade, at Saint Agnes, we heard about the fire
that broke out in Chicago, in a school like ours. The children
died at their desks, we heard. The school
was called Our Lady of the Angels, brick on the outside, wood,
all wood, within. Only one fire escape. They were trapped.
The firemen found that the gate in the fence was locked.

The seven foot iron fence , the south way in, was locked.
The inside of the school tasted fine to the fire.
Stairwells, walls, doors, and roof – all wood.
Only two fire alarm switches in the whole school.
Kindergarten to eighth grade, sixteen hundred children
second floor classrooms cut off by fire.They were trapped.

When did the children realize they were trapped?
When did the nuns recall the gate was locked?
Sparked in the cellar, chewing its way up, fire
fed on floors coated with wax on wood,
thirty eight years of wax on wood, a Catholic school
with wings and classrooms added on for the children

of Irish, German, Italian children, then children
of the veterans back from World War II, children trapped
on the second floor, who sat and prayed, locked
in the heat and smoke, the tongues of fire
pushed them up to foot high sills of wood
where small ones could not reach, trampled under by school

students bigger, who jumped, or fell out of school
windows. When the firemen got there , they saw children
from second floor windows, saw classrooms explode in fire.
Back home, we wondered if our gates were locked,
if we, on the fourth floor of our school, would be trapped
if fire caught hold of our floors of tile and wood.

Room two twelve, twenty-eight ten year olds burn like wood,
same age as me and my classmates at Saint Agnes School

three states to the East, same mixture of children
with names like Dunn, Campanale, Karwacki, and Gasteier,
trapped,
burned, the same age as me, with the gate locked,
their many futures exploding in fire.

And the fire finds the wood.
And the children leave the world.

SAFE HOUSE

Marooned

The sick woman floats on a narrow mattress
on a desert island,
in an ocean of grey floor, pale green walls.
The plane has crashed.
She's washed up
stranded here,
cast away into a wilderness
of dehydrated silence.
Dissociated .
Her blurred eyes cast about
for signs of health,
for signs of death.
But she's a castaway,
shipwrecked by broken bowels,
by waterstarved heart.

Companion Radio,
The franchised station
plays in the nursing home
where she lies, melting into the bed.
Plays in her fading ear:
Blessed Assurance, Jesus is mine…
As you are once a whiner
Still I'll cling to the old rugged cross…
Drugged across
I come to the garden alone…
The guard , a lone aide
Rock of Ages, cleft for me…
Crock of angels, left for me to entertain
When we've been there ten thousand years…
Towels and tears
Is what she hears.

BE THAT AS IT MAY,

I did dream about
confessing my sins
to the old Polish priest
with the strong voice,
questioning eyes.
A tall trunk reeked with welcome,
a perfume like peonies.
At some point I realized
that I had lost my clothes.
But it was May then,
the rains had encouraged
the bindweed and pokeweed,
the teasel and tearthroat,
the crabgrass and plantain
to grow lush and lustful,
crowding the garden
with their waving tendrils.
So I begged him to loose me of my strife,
the bonds of my blank eyes,
to set free the tears still trapped
under twenty years of leaves.

BURNED WHILE BAKING

We forget this about fire –
that it grabs on so fast
to what it's burning.
My left forearm touches the bread pan-
three hundred seventy-five degrees
for two seconds on the human arm-
flash of pain and quick removal
but already the burn hangs on
leaves a rose colored almond shape
and ache.
It's all energy
all change
drives out moisture out of the wood,
eats everything that's not already fire.
Then it starts to burn on the outside
until wood becomes fire.
Incandescent inflamed the blistering change.

GIVE ME A SPELL

to prize my eyes,
the blind girl cries.
It's rude to pry,
but what about prizing some sight from dead retinas?
what about prizing the ring from dead hand?

The spell should be contained in wetting solution,
released by hurling it like a football, or
casting it like a fishing line:

Triple triple coil and stipple
Golden light for salmon nipple
Eye of kestrel, toe of cat
Wool of milkweed, fist of fat
Come release her from her pain
Come and make her see again

The Shutting

Claudere, to shut off...
lights, music, conversation, engine...
close in on the stuffy silence in
the closed up car,
the dust mites dancing in the dark bedroom.

Occluded,oh clogged up eyes with the pollen of morning
which blots vision so that she fails to
include the aspirin with the other morning pills, and
exclude the warnings from worried friends,
that she must take these round white pills to
preclude another heart attack.
So she climbs into her clothes
with arteries shut out of the daylight.

GOING TO THE SUN HIGHWAY

In the dream,
I ride in a Jeep with two maintenance men.
We drive along a narrow dirt road
on a cliff
on "Going to the Sun Highway"
in Glacier National Park.
A huge, deep chasm screams below us.
Then, the road takes us over a one-lane stone bridge
across this chasm – no guard rails.
We pull over to the side of the road to get our breaths,
and an SUV comes toward us.
My driver calls to the driver of the jeep " terrible drive!"
and the other says " Oh, it gets worse."
We reach a place where another stone bridge
crosses another chasm,
but this one is too narrow for cars;
people have to cross it on foot.
I start out.
Part of the bridge is suspended
by criss-crossed white plastic clothesline.
I clutch those lines to cross part way,
but for the rest, I must walk without railings.
I try to close my eyes so I can't see the chasm below,
but I need to watch my steps.
This would be an easy place to let myself fall and die,
but something in me , a stubborn shrieking cat –
will not let me go.
I reach the other side, as the melting ice
slithers down the shale,
as the pines conceal the sun.
I pass young men and women approaching
and call out to them
Beware!
But I speak in a language they don't recognize.

Sonnet on a Line from Dylan Thomas

Let fall the tear of time, the sleeper's eye
will tear the dreams of dramas unrehearsed;
will twitch upon the inward eye of verse
that everyone's forgotten but the rhyme.
The sleeper's retina records the scene
of tears and thunder raining on a room
torn down in life but sparkling on the screen
that's lit within the sleeper's fevered brain.
A creek where clotted foliage of fall
provided brown protection for the wren,
where timing saved the swallows from the sky
reflected in the surface's teary plane.
The waking eye will fall upon the bare
dry creekbed birdless in the time dried air.

IKTSUARPOK

Is it the conference room,
the interrogation room,
or the confessional?
The name and furniture
make a difference.

As a spy would say in Inuit:
Iktsuarpok-
Go outside to check if anyone is coming

Morning yelps with cold.
The horseman winds through the forest-
how does he find his way through the trees?
In Magritte, the woman rides
through the trees.
The painter sets her free of gravity and physics.
In paintings we are set free from color and weight
we become whatever we wish.
The rich man gets into heaven,
up by the mother and child,
the saint shows up on the flight into Egypt.

I was sure I would meet him again
in the unfolding of the years, but oh, not on this side of death,
not on this side
of the lengthening shadows
on the green July lawn
that will not recede into light,
but will proceed into night,
inexorable, unknowable.

When the magical hills beyond reach
turn from green to blue
to purple,
all the hills like paintings of hills
purple in deep evening haze.

In the foreground the hunters on horseback like pilgrims
at a vigil, holding torches as they wait for the fox,
for the sound of the hounds.
Smell the purple night descending.
Smell the fire in the air, the rising breath of earth ascending
through pure space in silent fair
even now, I am only partly here.
Always in danger of the mind drifting away from the body
Going into yesterday or tomorrow or some deep inside,
apophatic thoughtless place,
charging on without a conscious thought.

Charging on
like the man in the story "To Build a Fire,"
unable to see the larger implications
of the situation,
and bound, therefore,
to freeze to death therein.
Is that my only witness value,
the value of a frozen body in the snow of history?

As the bone structure reappears,
the madwoman locked in the attic
keeps banging on the door for attention.

ACKNOWLEDGMENTS

Grateful acknowledgment is made to the following publications.

Barefoot Review, "Oriented"
The Centrifugal Eye, "Rules for Action in the Garden"
Common Ground Review, "Marooned"
Commonthought Magazine, "An Active and Personal Devil"
The Gunpowder Review, "Blue-winged Teal"
Lalitaimba, "Angry Enough to Die"
Life in Me Like Grass on Fire MWA Anthology, "Hearing Yesterday"
NCR, "October in Emmitsburg"
Scribble, "Everyone's Gone to the Moon"
Umbrella Journal, "The Hue of My Shoe"

About the Author

Anne Higgins teaches at Mount Saint Mary's University in Emmitsburg, Maryland. She is a member of the Daughters of Charity. Her poems have appeared in *Commonweal, Yankee, Spirituality and Health, The Centrifugal Eye,* and a variety of small magazines. Garrison Keillor has read two of her poems on "The Writers Almanac" – on 10/8/01 and 8/8/10. She is the author of six previous collections of poetry.

www.ingramcontent.com/pod-product-compliance
Lightning Source LLC
LaVergne TN
LVHW091203080426
835509LV00006B/808

* 9 780692 300046 *